AMAZING CLASSIC CARS
Coloring Book

Email: targetingtriumph@gmail.com

Thank you! Please leave a review, comment, and suggestion to improve our products.

Copyright ©2020
All rights reserved. No part of the publication may be reproduced, stored in a retrieval system, or transmitted in any form or by any means, electronic, mechanical, photocopying, recording or otherwise, without the prior written permission of the publisher.

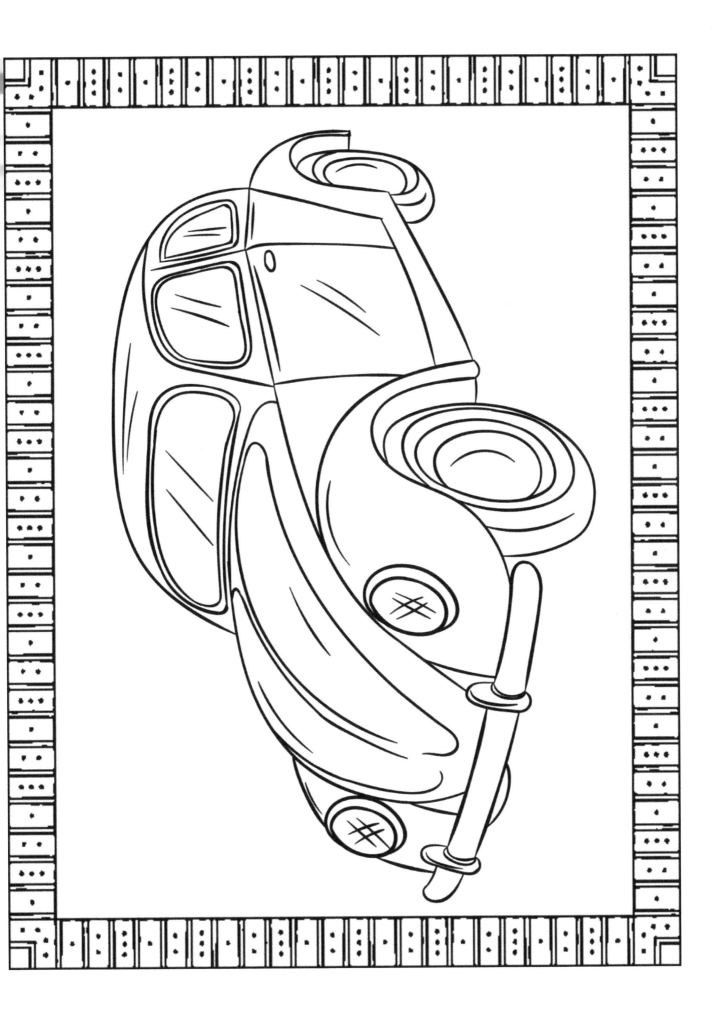

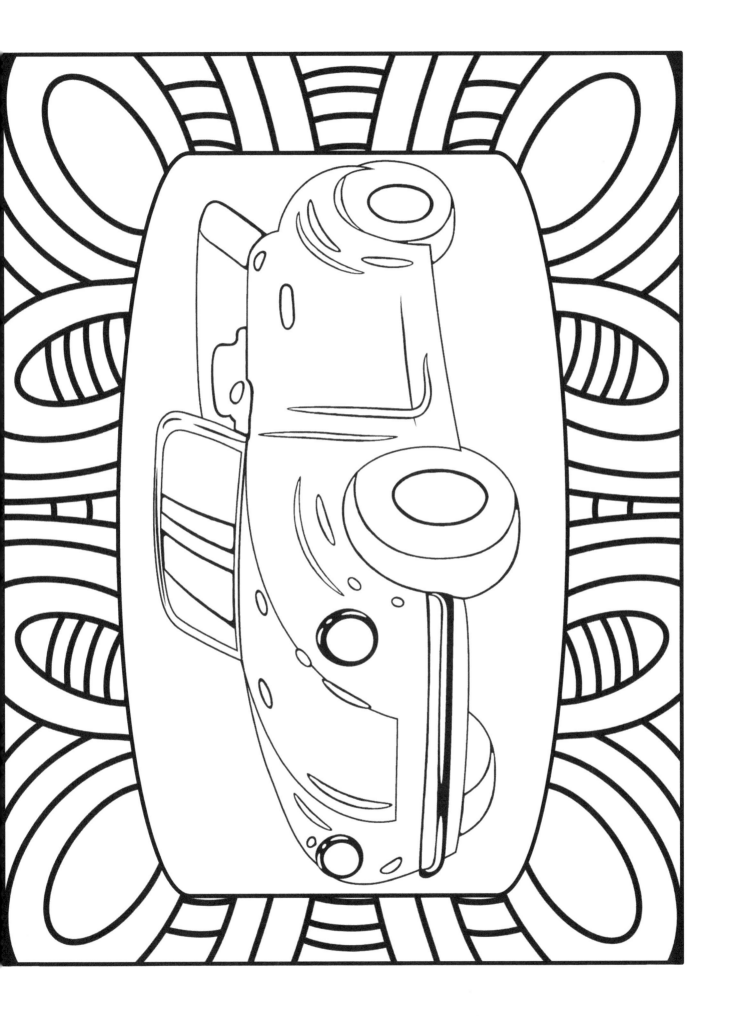

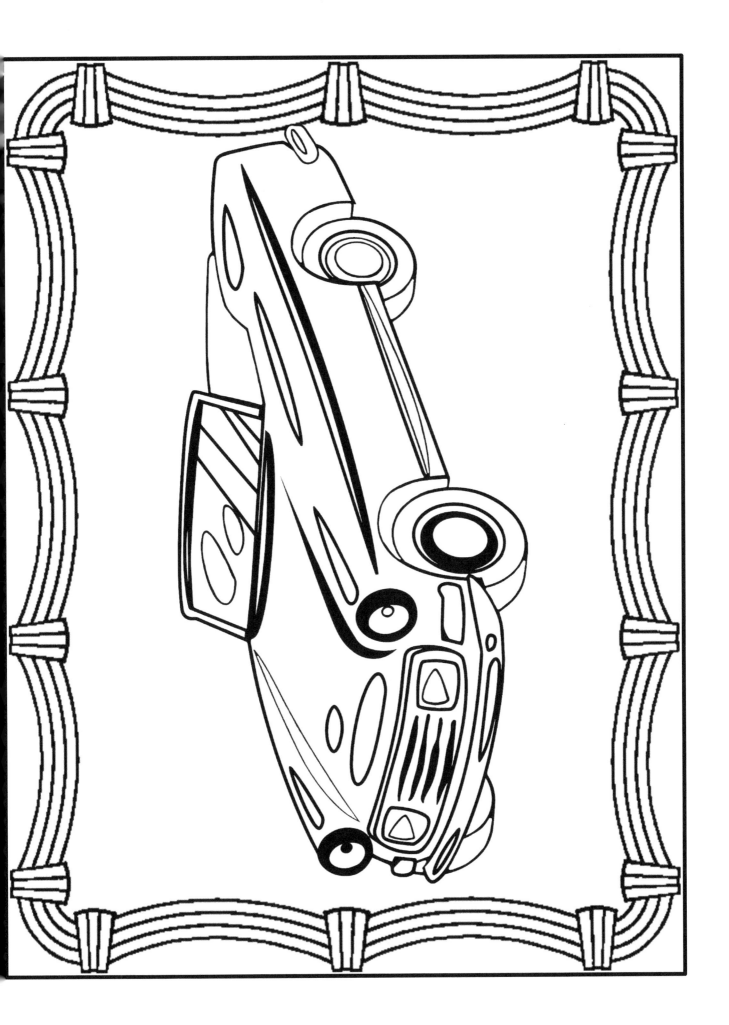

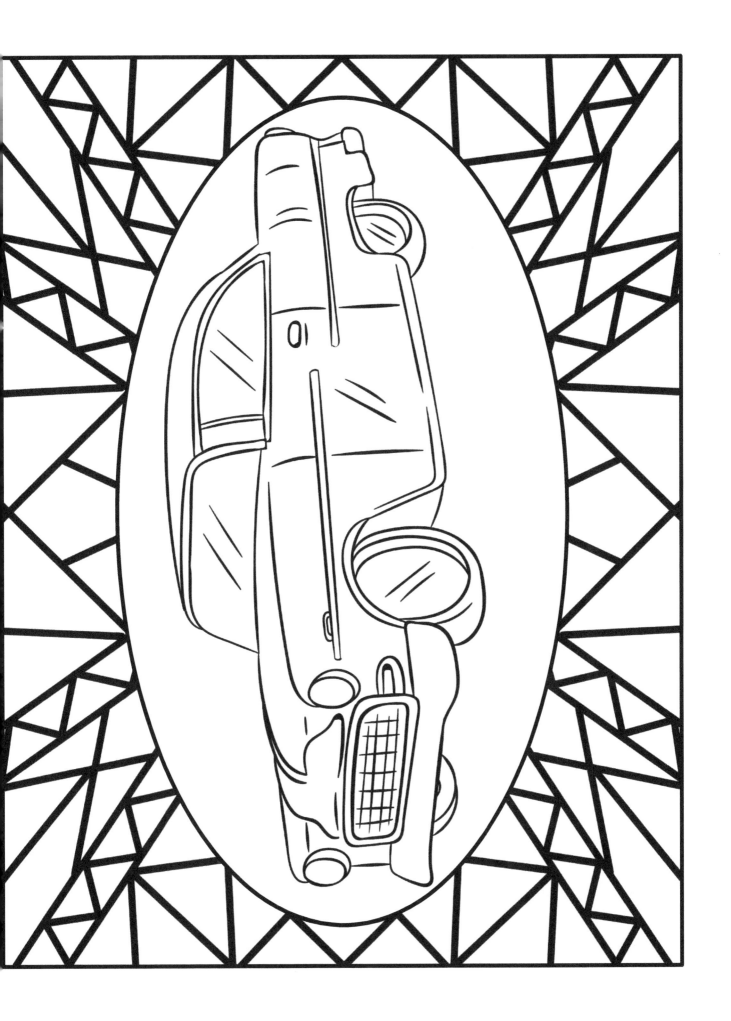

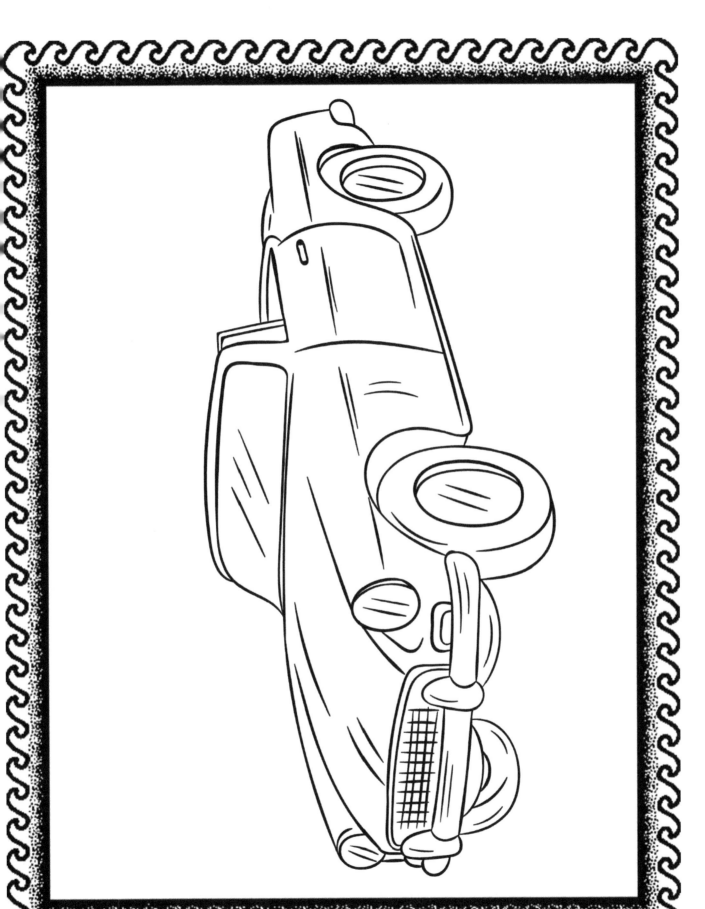

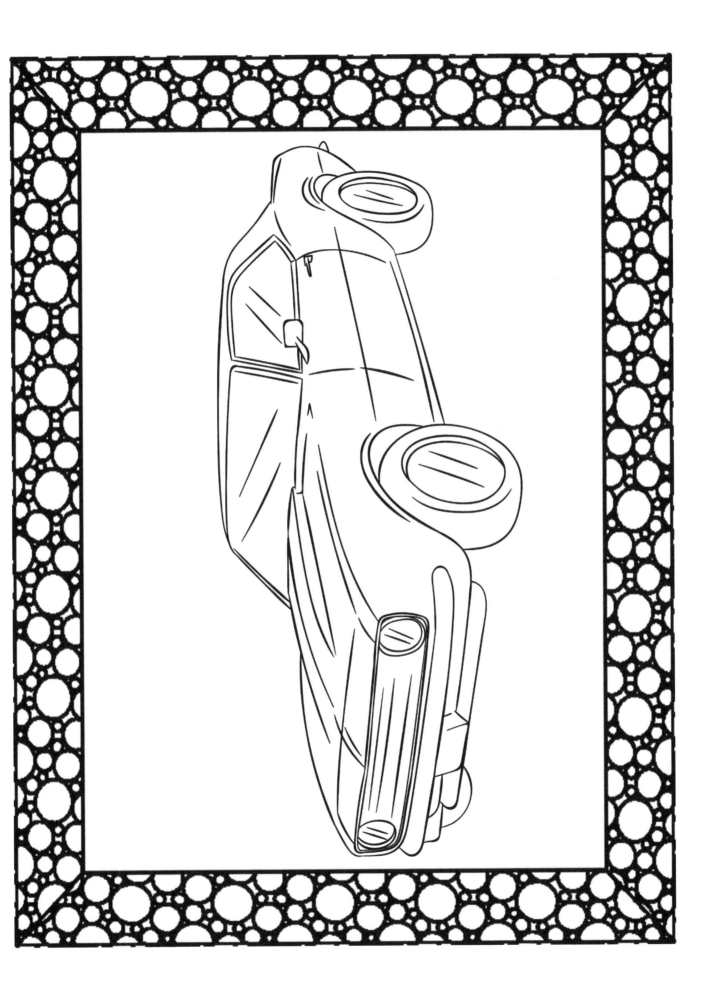

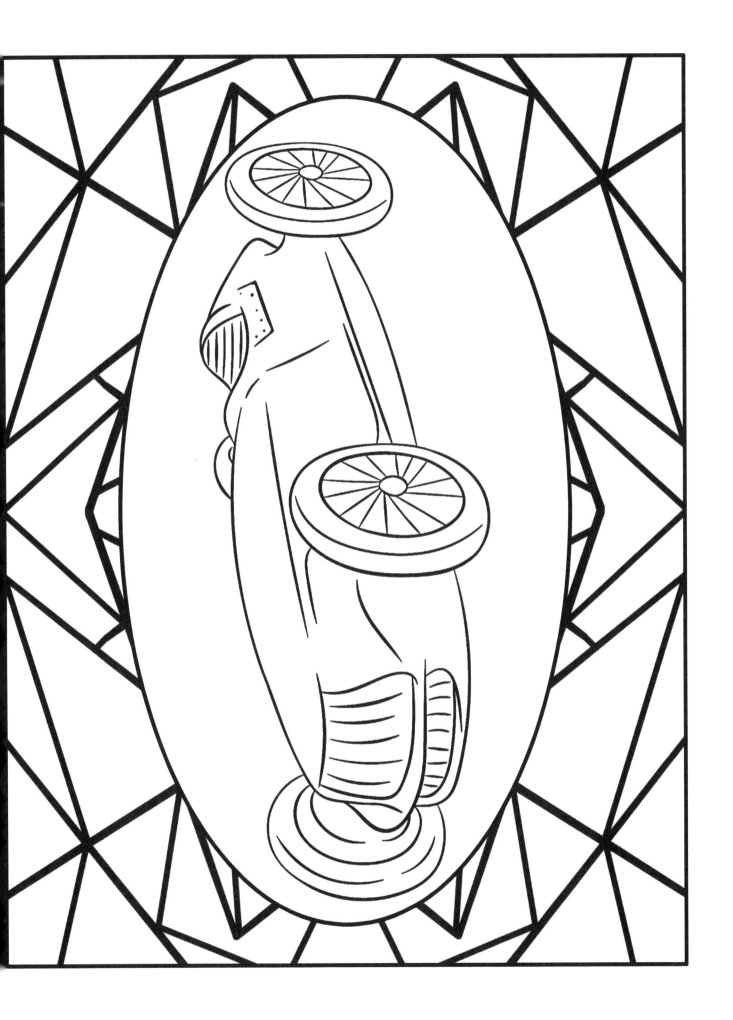

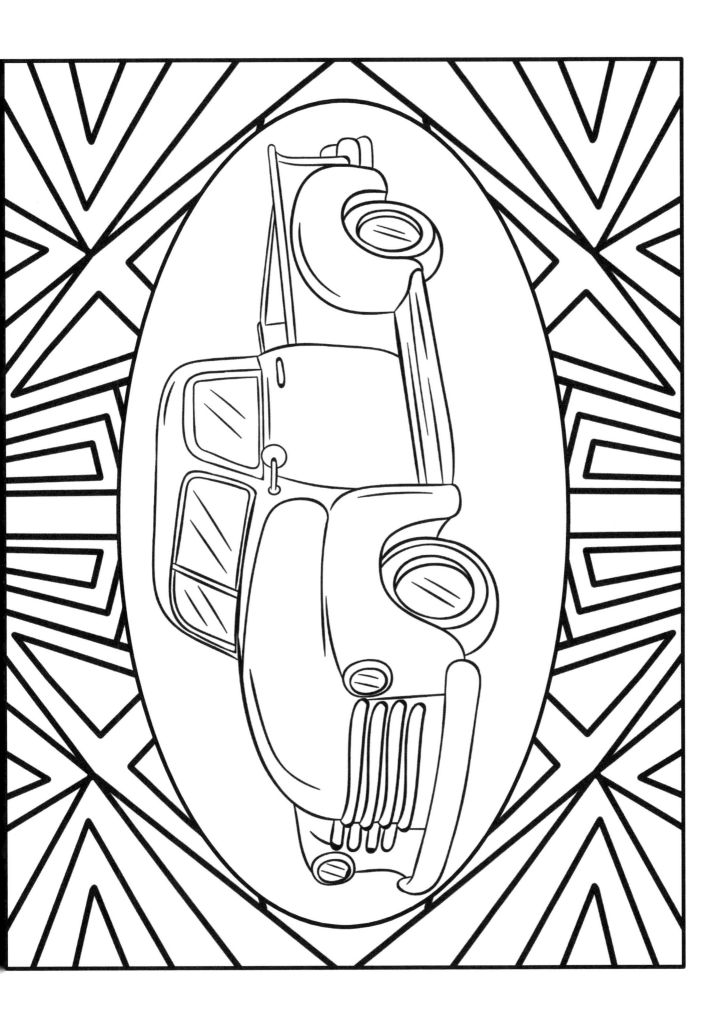

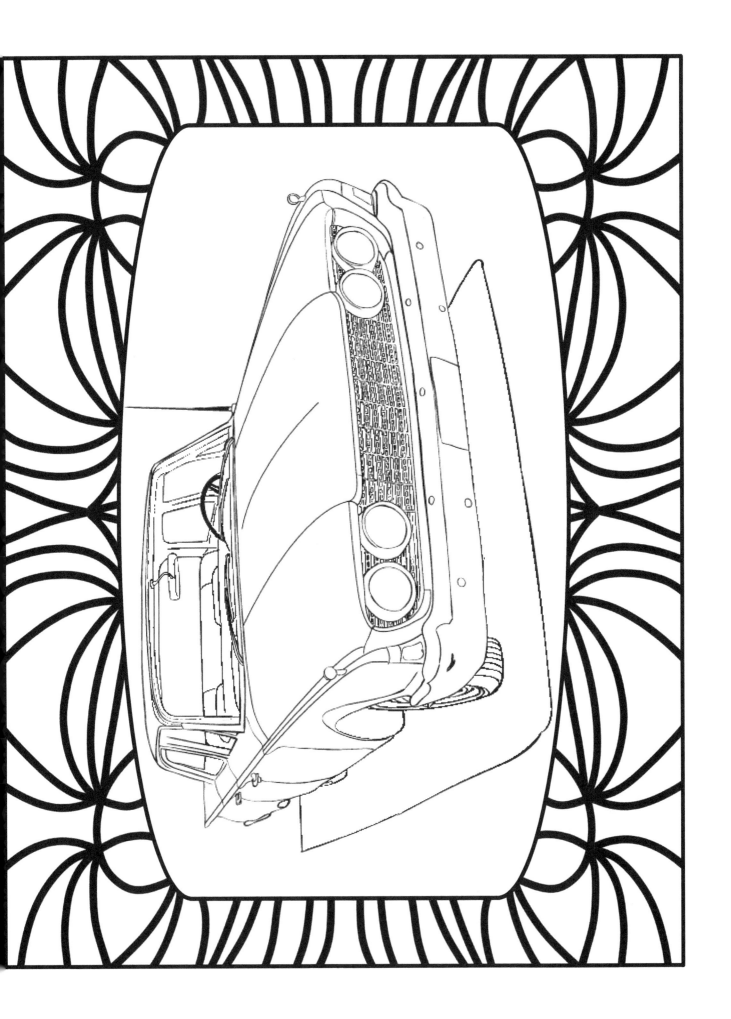

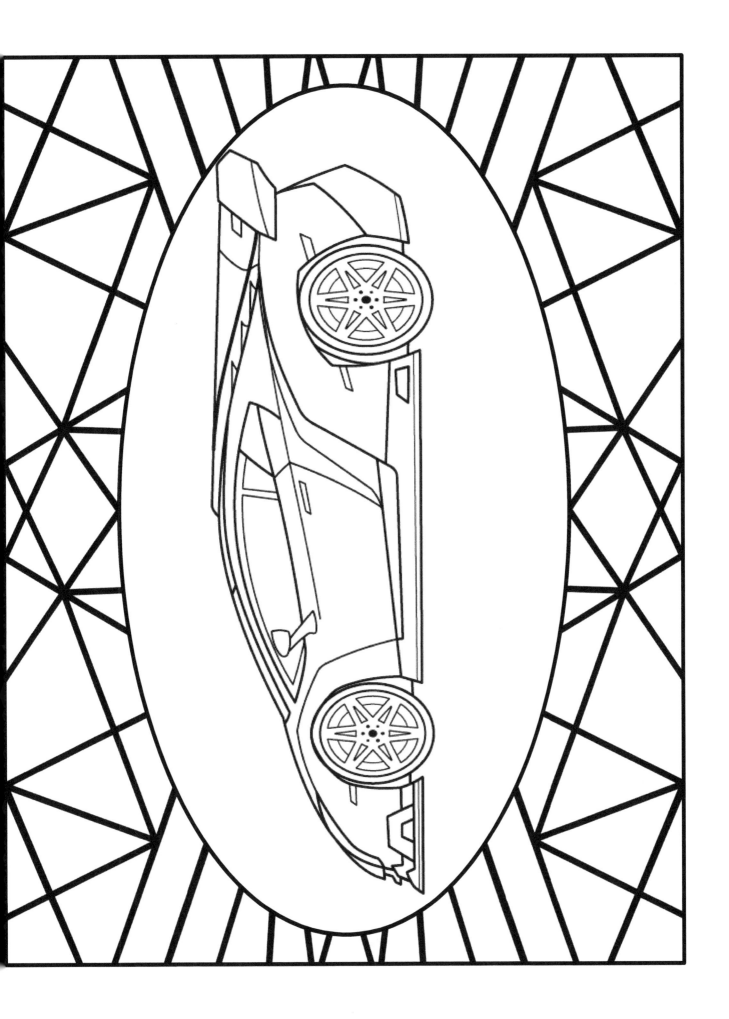

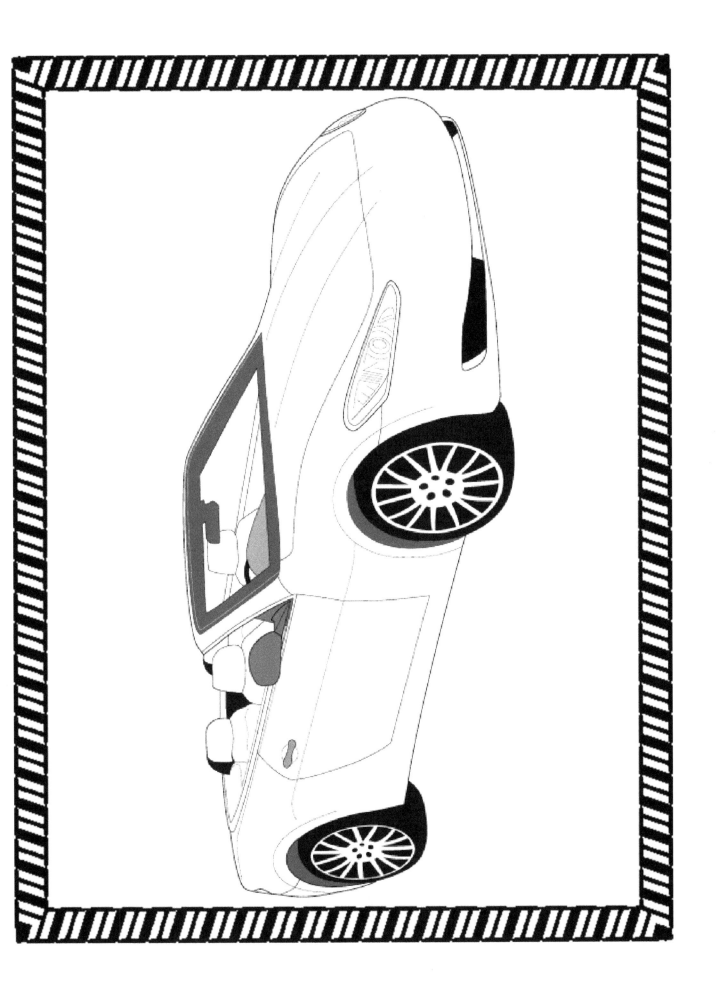

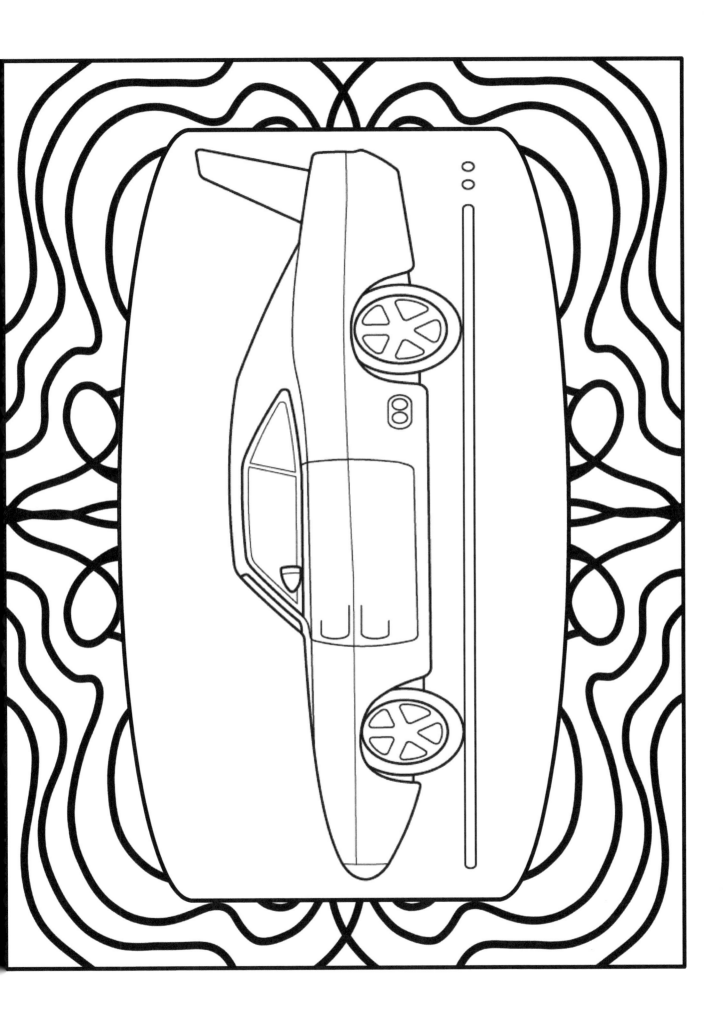

www.ingramcontent.com/pod-product-compliance
Lightning Source LLC
Chambersburg PA
CBHW082211161224
19129CB00014B/1005

9 798654 548863